JUMP
FOR PROFIT

by Peter May

ISBN 0-900611-99-5

Raceform Ltd.,
Compton, Newbury, Berkshire, RG20 6NL.

Edited: Graham Wheldon

ACKNOWLEDGEMENTS

Many thanks to Sara Howes, Mike Fincham, David Rossiter and Richard Lowther for their helpful comments and ideas.

Published: Raceform Ltd., Compton, Newbury, Berkshire, RG20 6NL.
Printed by: Greenshires Print Ltd., Kettering, Northants.

CONTENTS

LIST OF TABLES

INTRODUCTION

The cursor flickered on the computer screen, and the machine posed the now familiar question: '*Print Results?*'. I responded by pressing the *y* key and the printer clicked into action. A few moments later I was looking at my first profitable betting system.

It was June 1986 and I had recently decided to abandon my attempt to find a winning formula for the casino game Blackjack which did not involve card-counting, and during the past two weeks I had entered the results of one season's novices' chase races into the computer. Historically the machine had only ever analysed agricultural data (apart from many thousands of Blackjack simulations) but now it was faced with an entirely different task.

The data which had been extracted from the Formbook greatly simplified the complexity of the race, with only the month, number of runners in the race, where the favourite and second favourite finished on their latest starts, the position of the favourite and second favourite in this race, and the starting prices of the two horses entered. Three betting variables were added automatically: return from the favourite backed to win, second favourite to win and second favourite each way. The aim was to find a combination of inputs which resulted in a positive return for one, or all, of the betting variables.

At first glance the system appeared very profitable. It highlighted well over one hundred bets per year and produced an average profit of over 30p per £1 staked. So further testing was thought unnecessary. Mistake number one. Instead, a more important issue needed to be addressed: how much money could I expect to win? A computer simulation was devised to answer this question and it predicted a *retirement* date for me of 1994. According to the computer, by 1994 I would have amassed sufficient money to allow me to leave work and live comfortably from the winnings produced by *the system*. The simulation was based on an initial stake of £10 (from a bank of £200) and would rise to a figure exceeding £1000 by 1994. But eight years seemed a long time to be tied to the office, I wanted to leave earlier. A simple solution presented itself - increase the initial stake. My normal bet size was between £25 and £50, but I would place £100 on the system bets. Mistake number two.

I had never anticipated the start of a new racing season with such optimism. After what seemed an interminable wait, my first betting opportunity finally arose on Saturday, August 2nd at Newton Abbot. The horse: Karnatak. The price: 13/8. The result: a comfortable success. The conclusion: easy money.

On the following Thursday I placed my second bet, and collected from my second winner (price 5/4). A fantastic start, and now I really believed that I had found a winning formula. The third bet lost. So did the fourth. And the fifth. The sixth, Lord Laurence, cruised into the lead at the fourteenth, but fell at the next, the penultimate fence. Obviously I had expected a few losers, a ratio of one winner to one loser in fact. But four consecutive losers came as quite a shock, and put me into the red. So for the next bet, St Colme at Cartmel, I decided to halve the stake. Mistake number three. St Colme won easily at evens.

The St Colme race had taught me a valuable lesson; back to £100 per bet. The next bet went down and I had lost over £230 within three weeks, substantially more than I was used to losing. I therefore decided to play a little more *carefully* in the future. After a great deal of form analysis I decided to ignore the next recommendation completely. It won at 8/13.

Another half stake on bet 10 which won at 11/4. At this point I was over £100 down (after tax), but had I kept to the system's guidelines and (level) staking plan, I would have been in profit by £124.

This pattern continued throughout the remainder of the season, and by the following summer I had lost money. By sticking to the rules of the system and staking plan, however, I would have made a profit of almost £2000, after tax, a fact which only served to deepen my disappointment.

I have recounted this sequence of events to illustrate how simple it is to lose money backing racehorses, even with a *winning* formula. The three crucial errors I made are easy to spot in retrospect. Further testing of the system would have increased my confidence in its ability to return a profit, and may have highlighted ways to reduce the likelihood of long losing runs. Increasing the stake way beyond my normal bet put additional strain on the whole process. A long losing run at half the usual stake is easier to *handle* than at twice the normal stake. The third mistake is unforgivable. Using my own judgement to determine whether I followed the system's advice only serves to introduce an additional bias into the procedure, effectively making the system redundant.

For the next six years I managed to run the system properly, and it produced a reasonable profit each season. However, the average return gradually decreased due to the bookmakers' awareness of the weakness the system was exploiting, and by 1995 it was no longer profitable. However, I have replaced the approach with many other equally profitable selection methods which I detail in the remainder of this book.

In Part I some general issues concerning the level of profitability of National Hunt racing in Great Britain are outlined as background data. The three main race categories: hurdles races, chases and National Hunt flat races are examined individually as well as age and race size profiles. Several profitable selection methods are presented in Part II. These approaches include methods based on beaten favourites, running styles, and the use of race times. Other issues covered include the effect of weight carried in handicap races and information which can be gleaned from an examination of the sire's record. The section concludes with a brief summary of the key points of system development.

Notation

Throughout this text the following notation will be used to illustrate returns from several bets: six bets with two winners at 3/1 and 5/1 would be summarised as follows:

Bets	Wins (%)	Return/£
6	2 (33.3)	0.67

In the above example, the six bets produced a return of £4 to a £1 stake (i.e. +3+5-1-1-1-1 = 4), therefore the average return per bet is 4 ÷ 6 (total return divided by the number of bets) = 0.67 (or 67p per £1 staked). It should be noted that a return of 0.09 would simply be sufficient to cover the cost of tax (at 9%), anything less would result in a loss for off-course bettors. Finally, all bets referred to throughout this book are win singles unless otherwise stated.

PART I

BACKGROUND DATA

BACKGROUND DATA

There are approximately 3,500 races run under National Hunt rules in Great Britain each season, and this figure excludes the many hundreds of Point to Point events which take place throughout the country. Although National Hunt racing is sometimes referred to as the *winter game*, the season now runs throughout the year. The requirement for the racing authorities to generate income at every possible opportunity, via betting levy and admission charges, has reduced the mid-summer break from seven weeks to just four days.

During the 1995/96 season 43 racecourses staged National Hunt racing. The figure would have been reduced by one in 1996/97; Nottingham racecourse will only be used for Flat racing, but Wolverhampton are due to recommence jumping. Such a large number of courses produces a wide variation in course configuration. For example, consider the two south Devon courses: Newton Abbot and Exeter. The former is a flat, tight, left-handed course suiting the type of horse which prefers racing up with the pace. In contrast, Exeter racecourse, located on the side of Haldon Hill offers an entirely different configuration: right-handed with a stiff uphill run-in of 300 yards. This variation in courses adds another dimension to race analysis, requiring the punter to determine whether his/her selection will be suited by the track in addition to the normal considerations of form and fitness etc. This is especially important for front runners, a feature which is discussed in detail in Part II.

Horses need to be at least three years old before they can race under National Hunt rules with the career of a Jumps racehorse tending to last longer than that of its Flat racing counterpart. Generally starting in novices' hurdle races, the National Hunt horse can then progress through handicap hurdle races to novices' chases and finally handicap chases. Naturally, this career path takes several seasons to complete, and as such the National Hunt horse races more often than the average Flat racing animal. This is the main attraction for many Jumps racing supporters. Unlike Flat racing, where the very best horses seldom race beyond their three-year-old season, the National Hunt champions return year after year to test their ability against the younger generations. Imagine the 1993 King George VI and Queen Elizabeth Diamond Stakes at Ascot attracting the 7 year old Nashwan, in addition to Generous, Salsabil, User Friendly and the 1993 Epsom Derby winner, Commander In Chief. Quite a race! This reluctance to race the best Flat horses later in life is understandable since their stud value would rapidly diminish should the animal fail to run up to its best. When comparing the potential prize money which could be won to stud values, racing a champion Flat horse beyond its three-year-old season is very much a long odds on gamble. However, this is no compensation for the Flat racing fan. Fortunately, though, such contests occur quite frequently in National Hunt racing. Take, for example, the 1995 King George VI Tripleprint Chase, run at Sandown due to the abandonment of Kempton. This race featured the 1995 Cheltenham Gold Cup winner: Master Oats; the top chaser in Ireland: Merry Gale; the winners of the King George VI race for the previous two seasons: Barton Bank and Algan;

and the favourite for the 1996 Cheltenham Gold Cup: One Man. The *Racing Post* described the race as 'a titanic contest'. It is no wonder that National Hunt followers become supporters of the horses as opposed to just observers of races.

This tendency for the National Hunt horse to race over more seasons and in more races means the race analyst has a greater volume of form with which to work. More form implies that the punter should be able to more accurately evaluate the animal's likes and dislikes, such as optimum going and race distance. Consequently, determining the horse most likely to win a race *should* be easier. However, this does not mean it is easier to make money. The bookmakers are also able to assess the chances of each runner more precisely, and as a result the prices on offer will reflect these better informed assessments. To illustrate this point, consider Table 1. This table shows the average price of all winners in National Hunt and Flat races for several seasons covering approximately 28,000 races in total:

Table 1: Average Starting Price of Winners by Number of Runners: All Grades of National Hunt and Flat Races

	Average Starting Price of Winners	
Runners	**National Hunt**	**Flat**
2-4	2.05	2.01
5-9	4.34	4.57
10-15	6.51	6.95
16+	8.57	9.83
All	**5.13**	**6.09**

Apart from to 2-4 runner fields, for which the difference is insignificant, the average price of the winner is less for National Hunt races than for Flat races. This reflects the improvement in the accuracy of race assessments. In other words there is less uncertainty in National Hunt races.

Fortunately, uncertainty still exists, and it is this uncertainty which leads to the opportunity to win money. In many games of chance, such as roulette, dice and the National Lottery, the uncertainty has been removed. Whilst the outcome of any one spin of the roulette wheel, roll of the dice, or drop of the lottery ball is unknown before the event, the probability of each outcome can be computed exactly. For example, with an unbiased dice, the probability of a six being thrown on the next roll is 1/6. This probability is mathematically defined and proven. With horseracing, even the reasonably well defined National Hunt racing, this probability remains inexact. It is this very fact which allows us to profit from the sport, providing we bet sensibly.

Some people find the above result surprising. How can the outcome of National Hunt races be easier to predict than the results of Flat races, after all the horses have the added problem of jumping fences? One answer to this question concerns the relative levels of difficulty associated with the races. In theory, the more difficult the sport or game of skill, the more likely it is to be dominated by the best players. Taken to an extreme, an event that requires no skill whatsoever and hence depends purely on luck, could be won by any of the competitors. However, an event of immense difficulty will only be won by those with the highest level of skill. Chess, for instance, is dominated by a few top players. Clearly, jumping 18 fences in a three mile steeplechase is more difficult than running over a straight five furlongs, requiring the runners to possess an acceptable level of speed as well as jumping fluency. Consequently, the more talented participants should dominate. To illustrate this point consider Table 2. This table details the percentage of winning favourites for National Hunt and Flat racing:

Table 2: Percentage of Winning Favourites by Number of Runners: All Grades of National Hunt and Flat Races

	Percentage of Winning Favourites	
Runners	**National Hunt**	**Flat**
2-4	51.5	54.4
5-9	37.2	36.3
10-15	32.2	27.8
16+	25.7	21.1
All	**36.0**	**31.8**

The theory seems to hold up, with the strike rate for Jumps favourites, at 36.0%, significantly higher than for Flat race favourites, at 31.8%. It is also interesting to note how the gap between the pairs of percentages seems to widen as the number of runners increases. This reinforces our theory since races with more runners are, in general, harder to win.

However, it is still difficult not to feel anxious as our selection approaches each hurdle or fence, with this level of anxiety seeming to increase in proportion to the size of bet. So, what is the chance of our selection falling? Based on an analysis of approximately 88,000 race performances, the proportion of fallers in all types of National Hunt racing is about 4.4%. This is surprisingly low, implying only 4 fallers every 10 races. The proportion for unseated rider is even less at 2.4%, and only 0.3% of runners are brought down. Therefore, in total, approximately 7% of runners fail to complete due to falling, unseating or being brought down.

Profitability

We have established that National Hunt racing is more reliable than Flat racing and that we should not worry unduly about our horse falling, but to what degree are these facts reflected in the prices offered by the bookmakers? The following table presents the average return per £1 staked for almost 88,000 race performances over Jumps:

Table 3: Average Return by Starting Price

Starting Price	Winners	(%)	Runners	Average Return/£1
Odds On	1200	(57.2)	2098	-0.07
Evens-2/1	2070	(35.7)	5791	-0.09
85/40-5/1	3319	(20.1)	16539	-0.10
11/2-10/1	1868	(10.0)	18646	-0.15
11/1-20/1	765	(3.9)	19512	-0.39
22/1-40/1	193	(1.5)	13044	-0.56
50/1+	55	(0.5)	12037	-0.74
Total	**9470**	**(10.8)**	**87667**	**-0.33**

From Table 3 we can see that by selecting horses at random in National Hunt races we could expect to lose approximately 33p per £1 staked. This is the result of the bookmakers' pricing policy. The average loss for Flat racing is approximately 30p per £1 staked (see *Flat Racing For Profit*, published by Raceform).

Although this loss of 33p per £1 staked is extremely high in relation to many casino games, it compares favourably with the National Lottery (50p per £1) and football pools betting at 70p per £1. Premium Bonds, on the other hand, offer a much safer bet with an average gain of 5p per £1 staked and no risk attached.

On the positive side, Table 3 reinforces the view that National Hunt racing is predictable. This is illustrated by the high correlation between the odds on offer and the strike rate. As the winners to runners strike rate increases, the odds decrease. If the outcome of the races were not predictable, by bookmakers and punters alike, such a strong relationship would not be apparent.

It is interesting to note from Table 3 that the average return for the higher priced horses is poorer than for the shorter priced animals. This simply reflects the greater degree of under pricing associated with these runners. In other words, in order to accurately mirror the true probability of success, most 33/1 shots should really be priced at 50/1 or greater. As the price decreases the discrepancy between the *fair* price and starting price diminishes. Therefore, restricting our random selection process to horses starting at 10/1 or less reduces the loss to just 10½p per £1 staked. Whilst a 25/1 shot may look an attractive betting option, these longer priced horses tend, in general, to offer poor value compared to the shorter priced animals.

Hurdle Races

Hurdle races constitute the majority of all National Hunt races, 54% in fact. Broadly speaking, these races are contested by ex-Flat race horses, and National Hunt bred animals for whom hurdling is merely a stepping stone to steeplechasing. Hurdle races can be conveniently categorised into four groups: *conditions races*, *novices' races*, *other non-handicap races* and *handicaps*. Conditions races are non-handicap events which include the best hurdle races staged each year, such as the Champion Hurdle and Stayers' Hurdle. In addition to the graded races, conditions events include contests for four year old second season hurdlers as well as trials for the championship races. Novices' hurdle races were, historically, for horses which had not won a hurdle race prior to the current season. However, due to the introduction of summer racing this condition was revised to not having won a hurdle race prior to the 1st May. Consequently, under the new conditions, horses could have won a hurdle race in the previous season and still qualify for novices' events in the current season. The category other non-handicap races refers to the remaining races for which horses are not allotted weights by the British Horseracing Board's (BHB) Handicappers. Therefore, this category includes, amongst others, selling, maiden and claiming races. Handicap races are weight adjusted events. Once qualified for a handicap the BHB's team of Handicappers rate the performances of the animal and evaluate its handicap mark. This mark will change as the season progresses and the horse runs in more races. The handicap mark determines the weight the horse is set to carry relative to the other runners in the race. The aim of the weight adjustment is to produce more competitive races by penalising the better animals. Handicap hurdle races (which include novices' handicaps, selling handicaps etc.), and the use of weight to slow horses down, is discussed in more detail in Part II.

The minimum distance of a hurdle race is two miles, with the longest race at a little over 3 miles 3 furlongs. Almost 60% of all hurdle races are over a distance of 16-18 furlongs with the runners expected to jump between 8 and 10 flights of hurdles. Less than 6½% of races are over a distance exceeding 3 miles, requiring the horses to jump at least 12 flights.

Horses aged three years and upwards are qualified for hurdle races. However, 44% of all runners are aged between five and seven years. This seemingly low average age range is simply due to a large proportion of hurdlers progressing to steeplechasing after one or two seasons over the smaller obstacles. The older hurdlers tend to be animals which are not suited, either physically or mentally, to fences. Table 4 shows the distribution of runners by age range for almost 7,000 races:

Table 4: Winners to Runners Strike Rate and Average Return for Hurdle Races: Age Range by Race Category

Age (yrs.)		Cond. Hdl.	Nov. Hdl.	Other Hdl.	Hcap. Hdl.	All Races
3	*W*	0	304	96	19	419
	R	0	3261	1012	90	4363
	Ret.	-	-0.41	-0.24	+0.39	-0.36
4	*W*	17	715	207	420	1359
	R	145	7305	2319	3447	13216
	Ret.	+0.18	-0.42	-0.48	-0.26	-0.38
5..7	*W*	64	1272	324	1584	3244
	R	344	13898	3656	12999	30897
	Ret.	-0.28	-0.44	-0.41	-0.16	-0.32
8..10	*W*	54	302	169	1138	1663
	R	398	4493	1981	13110	19982
	Ret.	-0.32	-0.60	-0.46	-0.32	-0.40
11..12	*W*	1	2	13	37	53
	R	20	45	97	880	1042
	Ret.	+0.70	-0.81	+0.16	-0.63	-0.54
13+	*W*	1	2	3	7	13
	R	7	11	22	176	216
	Ret.	-0.36	+0.82	-0.62	-0.72	-0.62
Total	***W***	**137**	**2597**	**812**	**3205**	**6751**
	R	**914**	**29013**	**9087**	**30702**	**69716**
	Ret.	**-0.20**	**-0.46**	**-0.42**	**-0.26**	**-0.36**

W indicates the number of winners, *R* the number of runners, and *Ret* the average return per £1 staked.

One of the most significant features revealed by Table 4 is the decline in average return for the older horses. Consider, for instance, those hurdlers aged 11 years and older: 1258 race performances resulted in only 66 wins, a strike rate of 5.2%. This compares to a strike rate of 9.8% for their younger opponents. However, this poorer strike rate is not reflected in higher prices offered by the bookmakers, hence the abysmal return per bet.

Specifically, a loss of 55p per £1 staked for the older animals compared to a loss of 36p per £1 staked for the younger runners. This illustrates the degree of poor value generally offered about older horses.

Another interesting feature is the profitable return from backing all runners aged three years taking part in handicap hurdle races. The average return of 39p per £1 staked reflects how much this type of runner is under rated, by the punters and bookmakers, resulting in odds which are, in fact, generous. Three-year-old hurdlers often will be considered too weak and inexperienced compared with their older rivals. Clearly, this judgement is misplaced, which is an error we can exploit.

With an average loss of 46p per £1 staked, novices' hurdle races would seem to offer the poorest betting medium. However, this loss can be explained, in part, by a higher than average number of runners per race, and more high priced runners than other types of hurdle race. In fact, novices' hurdle races are, in general, easier to assess with a winners to runners strike rate for favourites of 44% over the past four seasons, compared to an average of 37% for all hurdle races for the same period. In terms of profit, backing all novices' hurdle race favourites since the 1992/93 season would have resulted in a loss of only 4p per £1 staked.

Chases

Although hurdle racing can be exciting at times, it is steeplechasing which usually provides the spectacle for National Hunt racing. If you are unsure about this statement, cast your thoughts back to the closing stages of the 1995 Mumm Melling Chase at Aintree. The three top 2 mile chasers, Viking Flagship, Deep Sensation and Martha's

Son, approached the final fence at full racing speed and jumped it in unison before battling out the finish with just a length separating the three at the line. That's *real* horseracing.

Chases make up approximately 42% of all National Hunt races and range in distance from 2 miles, requiring the horses to possess speed and jumping fluency, to the 4½ miles of the Grand National where the emphasis is on stamina.

To facilitate meaningful analyses, chases have been broken down into five categories. The first four: *conditions races*, *novices' races*, *other non-handicap* races and *handicaps*, are the same as for hurdle races with the same definitions. The fifth category is *hunter* chases. These events are for horses which have been classified as hunters during the hunting season and are restricted to amateur riders.

An initial analysis of chases by race category and number of runners reveals several interesting trends. Consider Table 5:

Table 5: Analysis of Chases by Number of Runners Within Race Category

Number of Runners		Cond. Chase	Nov. Chase	Other Chase	Hcap. Chase	Hunter Chase	All Races
2..4	*W*	51	269	13	526	36	895
	R	183	994	48	1893	129	3247
	Ret.	-0.07	-0.25	-0.15	-0.09	-0.30	-0.15
5..7	*W*	54	661	45	1243	133	2136
	R	312	4000	276	7375	811	12774
	Ret.	-0.23	-0.27	-0.29	-0.16	-0.32	-0.21
8..12	*W*	16	628	58	882	226	1810
	R	156	6008	541	8304	2158	17167
	Ret.	-0.36	-0.38	-0.25	-0.22	-0.42	-0.30
13..16	*W*	4	122	19	144	96	385
	R	60	1737	278	2016	1347	5438
	Ret.	-0.60	-0.46	-0.50	-0.31	-0.47	-0.41

17+	*W*	0	12	9	41	20	82
	R	0	215	170	813	402	1600
	Ret.	-	-0.38	-0.54	-0.32	-0.64	-0.43
Total	***W***	**125**	**1692**	**144**	**2836**	**511**	**5308**
	R	**711**	**12954**	**1313**	**20401**	**4847**	**40226**
	Ret.	**-0.25**	**-0.35**	**-0.34**	**-0.20**	**-0.43**	**-0.28**

W indicates the number of winners, *R* the number of runners and *Ret* the average return per £1 staked.

Clearly, as the number of runners per race increases so does the bookmakers' over-round. This is a trend which is continued through both codes of racing, Flat and Jumps, and as mentioned in the previous section, it accounts for the poor return for novices' hurdle races. Hunter chases seem to offer a very poor average rate of return, with a loss of 43p per £1 staked, which is, in fact, worse than the National Lottery when the effect of tax is added. Unusually, this poor return is maintained in the very small fields. From Table 5 it can be seen that in fields of 2-4 runners the average loss for handicap chases is 9p per £1 staked, whereas for hunter chases the figure is 30p per £1, a huge difference.

A reason for this poor rate of return can be found by examining the price profile of the hunter chase runners. These races usually feature a large proportion of horses with very little chance of winning, probabilities which are not accurately reflected by the odds on offer (i.e. long shots still under priced, illustrated by Table 3). Consequently, the bookmakers' over-round is increased. However, the hunter chase category has the highest proportion of winning favourites, at a little over 48%, compared to 46% for novices' chases and figures in the mid 30s for the other categories. In fact, simply backing all hunter chase favourites over the past few seasons would have returned a profit of 7p per £1 staked, before tax. All other race types produced a loss of between 3p and 23p per £1 staked.

The average age range of a chaser is 8 to 10 years old. As with the hurdlers, the older chasers win less frequently than the younger horses and this poor strike rate is not reflected in higher prices offered by the bookmakers. Chasers aged up to 10 years old have a winners to runners strike rate of 14% and an average loss of 25p per £1 staked. In comparison, the strike rate for older horses, 11 years and upwards, is only 8% and the average return is a loss of 44p per £1 staked. Clearly, the age of the animal is a factor which should be carefully considered before placing a bet.

National Hunt Flat Races

National Hunt Flat races are designed to give National Hunt bred horses experience of racing before they attempt hurdles or fences. These races attract a high bookmakers' over-round with a random selection producing an average loss of 47p per £1 staked over the past few seasons. This level of under pricing is due in part to the fact that a large proportion of the runners are unknown quantities, and the bookmakers are not prepared to take any chances about this type of horse. To illustrate this point, by selecting horses at random in the 11/2-10/1 price band for all types of National Hunt race would return a loss of 15p per £1 staked. For Bumpers this loss is an incredible 30p per £1 staked.

As a result of such prohibitive pricing, identifying profitable betting strategies for National Hunt Flat races is an extremely difficult task.

Summary

In this section I have tried to show the degree to which the odds are stacked in favour of the bookmakers, and how the average rate of return varies depending on the number of runners in the race, the starting price, and age of the horse. Whilst the starting price provides a good guide to the chance of success there are instances where it severely underestimates the true odds of runners, most notably the older horses. We have also seen one case, three year old horses running in handicap hurdle races, where the average starting price exceeds a fair price providing a profitable betting opportunity.

In the following section, we concentrate on developing selection methods which should result in a positive return. We have already seen that on average the bookmaker bets to an over-round of 33% per race, and has at his/her disposal all the information available to the general public. Therefore, using conventional methods for selecting horses (i.e. checking the suitability of the going, race distance etc.) is unlikely to return a profit. For the off-course punter to make a long term profit by evaluating races in the traditional way, either the bookmaker needs to make an appalling mistake or the punter needs to be exceptionally talented at analysing races. To put the level of skill required into perspective, the top professional gamblers only make 10p to 15p per £1 staked. Consequently, the best route to a profitable return is to adopt an unconventional approach to racehorse selection and consider information which is often overlooked by the bookmaker, and other punters. This type of approach to betting is examined in Part II.

PART II

SELECTION METHODS FOR JUMP RACING

SELECTION METHODS FOR JUMP RACING

In this section we examine various facets of National Hunt racing and develop several profitable selection methods. The section starts with an analysis of recent form and the importance of the animal's starting price on its previous race.

Recent Form and Beaten Favourites

Recent form is treated as one of the most important aspects of race analysis. In almost every book aimed at providing the reader with methods for picking winners there will be a section relating to recent form. Usually the author will suggest that the punter ensures that his/her selection has 'good recent form' before placing a bet. However, defining *good* or *poor* recent form is not an easy task. A guide, though, can be gleaned from considering the distance the horse was beaten on its latest run. Table 6 illustrates the relationship between the chance of success and the distance the horse was beaten on its latest run:

Table 6: Average Return and Strike Rate by Distance Beaten Last Time: All Grades of National Hunt Races

Distance† Beaten Last Time	Winners	(%)	Runners	Average Return/£1
0	2070	(25.5)	8121	-0.12
0.01-2.0	515	(20.6)	2495	-0.16
2.01-5.0	687	(18.7)	3677	-0.15
5.01-10.0	856	(16.2)	5286	-0.16
10.01-20.0	1140	(12.2)	9320	-0.25
20.01+	1626	(6.6)	24599	-0.41
Not Complete	721	(6.0)	11971	-0.46
Unraced‡	1855	(8.4)	22208	-0.37
Total	**9470**	**(10.8)**	**87667**	**-0.33**

† distance beaten is given in horse lengths. ‡ unraced this season

As you may expect, the above table does not reveal a profitable betting strategy, but it does provide some valuable information. The most interesting feature of Table 6 is the decline in strike rate *and* average return as the distance beaten increases. In other words, the starting price does not reflect the lower probability of success of those horses well beaten last time.

A second component of recent form which should be considered is the price the horse started for its latest race. We have already seen that the starting price of a horse provides a good guide to its chance of success (see Table 3). This trend is maintained for the price the animal started on its latest run and is particularly significant for novices' hurdle races. Table 7 combines starting price and distance beaten last time for almost 2,000 novices' hurdle races:

Table 7: Average Return by Distance Beaten and Starting Price Last Time: Novices' Hurdle Races

Distance† Beaten Last Time		Odds On	Evens-2/1	85/40-5/1	11/2-10/1	11/1+	All Prices
		Starting Price Last Time					
0	*W*	122	125	172	87	39	545
	R	367	422	625	357	254	2025
	Ret.	-0.18	-0.01	-0.09	-0.20	-0.28	-0.13
0.01-2.0	*W*	16	44	53	27	21	161
	R	56	121	225	196	175	773
	Ret.	-0.19	+0.33	-0.13	-0.53	-0.49	-0.25
2.01-5.0	*W*	10	36	57	53	47	203
	R	35	120	283	255	310	1003
	Ret.	+0.03	-0.09	-0.25	-0.18	-0.29	-0.22
5.01-10.0	*W*	21	33	86	74	56	270
	R	55	113	390	394	534	1486
	Ret.	+0.13	+0.35	-0.04	-0.20	-0.47	-0.20
10.01+	*W*	14	56	145	171	291	677
	R	71	275	1128	1819	7925	11218
	Ret.	-0.34	-0.03	-0.30	-0.35	-0.64	-0.54
Not Complete	*W*	8	12	32	36	39	127
	R	28	74	267	368	2581	3318
	Ret	-0.28	-0.36	-0.49	-0.04	-0.70	-0.60
Total	***W***	**191**	**306**	**545**	**448**	**493**	**1983**
	R	**612**	**1125**	**2918**	**3389**	**11779**	**19823**
	Ret.	**-0.17**	**+0.03**	**-0.22**	**-0.28**	**-0.63**	**-0.46**

W indicates the number of winners, *R* the number of runners and *Ret* the average return per £1 staked. † distance beaten is given in horse lengths.

Several interesting features are exhibited in Table 7. Firstly, the average return remains reasonably constant for horses beaten up to 10 lengths but drops markedly to a loss of 54p per £1 staked for horses beaten over 10 lengths on their previous run, and to a loss of 60p for those which failed to complete last time. Secondly, for runners which started at odds against on their previous start there is a steady decline in the average return as this price increases. And for animals which started at over 10/1 most recently the average return drops to a very poor loss of 63p per £1 staked. These are clearly horses to avoid.

However, profitable selection methods are also appearing, notably horses beaten on their last start by less than 10 lengths whilst starting at 2/1 or less. From Table 7, we can see that this approach would have resulted in 160 winners from 500 races, a strike rate of almost 32% with a return of 13p per £1 staked.

In Part I we found that the higher priced horses generally offer poorer value. Removing the horses which started at 10/1 or higher and applying the restrictions outlined above decreases the number of bets by 70 to 430 at the expense of only one winner. The strike rate improves to 37% with a return of 28p per £1 staked. Therefore,

> *consider backing any horse starting at less than 10/1 in a novices' hurdle race which, on its latest start, was beaten no more than 10 lengths at a starting price of 2/1 or less: expected profit 28p per £1 staked.*

This selection method involves a fair amount of searching through past histories, but fortunately it can be simplified by restricting the horses eligible for selection to beaten favourites. Both of the trade papers indicate beaten favourites in the race card reducing the amount of searching required. Therefore,

> *consider backing any horse starting at less than 10/1 in a novices' hurdle race which, on its latest start, was a beaten favourite finishing within 10 lengths of the winner: expected profit 25p per £1 staked.*

There is only a slight difference in the expected return and number of bets for these two selection methods, and as mentioned earlier the second approach should be easier to implement.

Weight Analysis

In horseracing, Jumps or Flat, the standard measure of ability is the official rating, also known as the handicap mark. Ultimately all horses receive a handicap mark assigned by a team of Handicappers employed by the BHB, whether they run in handicap races or not. The rating is a convenient way of expressing the superiority of one animal relative to another. For example, a horse rated 85 would be considered to possess more ability than an animal rated 70. For handicap races, this rating determines the amount of weight each horse will carry. In the previous example, the horse rated 85 would carry 15 lbs. more weight than the horse rated 70. It should be noted that the handicap marks do not determine the *amount* of weight to be carried, just the weight one horse will carry relative to another. Consequently, it would be possible for these two horses to be set to carry 11-04 (11 stone 4 lbs.) and 10-03 in one race, and 11-10 and 10-09 in another race on the same day. The absolute weight carried is determined by the BHB rating of the highest rated horse in the race. In these two hypothetical races, the top rated horse in the first race would be rated higher than the top rated horse in the second race.

This is an important distinction to make, and it is imperative to remember that a horse carrying 12-0, for instance, is not necessarily badly handicapped. Likewise, an animal set to carry 10-0 is not guaranteed to be well handicapped. The weight carried by a horse simply reflects the strength of the race. Just because a handicapper is set to carry 12-0 is no reason to assume it cannot win.

There are occasions when runners in handicaps carry more weight than their official rating requires. This can happen when the rating requires the animal to carry a weight which is below the minimum set for the race. The minimum weight is normally 10-0 although it can be increased to 10-04 or 10-07 for certain races. In such cases horses which are *out of the handicap* effectively carry overweight. For example, if the top weight in a race was set to carry 11-10 and was rated 120, a horse rated 80 should only carry 8-08 but would have to carry the minimum weight, 10-0, an overweight of 20 lbs. These horses are generally considered to be badly handicapped.

Official ratings have most effect in handicap races. The aim of handicaps is to give all horses the same chance of winning by penalising the better animals by giving them more weight to carry. Consequently, many gamblers do not find handicap races a viable betting medium. For instance, in the book *Braddock's Complete Guide to Horse Race Selection and Betting* (Longman, 1983), Peter Braddock recommends that handicaps *"must not be considered for serious purposes of selection".* This is a rather extreme view, although it did discourage me from betting in handicaps for many years.

However, in *Betting For A Living* (Aesculus Press, 1992), Nick Mordin suggests that weight carried should be ignored when assessing form and provides evidence from this, and the previous century, to support the claim. At first I dismissed this idea without a second thought. However, I am beginning to believe that it may have some validity. We should be able to test this theory using independent handicap ratings as provided by organisations such as Timeform and Raceform. If Mordin's contention is true, there should be no difference between the winners to runners strike rate for the top rated selections after adjusting for weight (the usual approach) and for the top rated selections without any weight adjustment. Analysing the ratings from an independent source for almost 800 handicap races produced the following results:

Strike Rate For	Weight Adjusted:	24%
Top Rated Horse	Weight Ignored:	23%

The minimal difference between the two percentages supports the hypothesis that weight carried has no effect. It also questions the value of high priced ratings services, especially since the top weight in Jumps handicap races regardless of its position in the ratings, wins on average 20% of races.

As a further check we can look at the winners to runners strike rate for all National Hunt handicap runners by weight carried. Again, if weight has a significant effect, and the Handicappers are reasonably accurate in their assessments, this profile should be uniform over the different weight categories. On the other hand, if weight has only a minimal effect, the better horses, carrying higher weights, should win more often. Consider Table 8 which illustrates the winners to runners strike rate for almost 6,000 handicap races:

Table 8: Winners to Runners Strike Rate by Weight Carried: All National Hunt Handicap Races

Weight Carried†	Winners	(%)	Runners
12-01+	27	(38.6)	70
11-08..12.00	1540	(16.7)	9218
11-00..11-07	1246	(13.6)	9181
10-08..10-13	1278	(12.1)	10594
10-00..10-07	1526	(9.1)	16711
..9-13	286	(6.6)	4306
All Weights	**5903**	**(11.8)**	**50080**

† weight carried includes claims by jockeys and overweight.

Clearly, the horses carrying most weight win more often which indicates that the handicapping process is not resulting in total uniformity. So perhaps Nick Mordin is correct, and for National Hunt races at least, we should not place too much emphasis on the effect of the amount of weight carried when assessing the chances of horses. And to base the assessment of the runners' abilities on the official ratings before adjustment for weight.

Another long held belief is that horses find it harder to carry weight on soft ground. Braddock comments: 'it is more difficult for horses to carry big weights on soft or heavy ground. Conversely, when the ground is firm ... top weights are more likely to prevail.' Mordin agrees with this statement, and it seems to possess a degree of logical merit. Table 9 shows the number of winners for almost 6,000 runners that carried 11-10 or more in a National Hunt handicap races, together with the difference from the *expected* number of winners:

Table 9: Winners to Runners Strike Rate by Going: All National Hunt Handicap Races

Going	Winners	(%)	Runners	Diff. From Expected	Adjusted Difference
Hard	5	(38.5)	13	2.0	68.9
Firm	110	(23.6)	466	23.3	26.9
Good to firm	276	(21.5)	1284	82.2	42.4
Good	298	(16.4)	1812	61.0	25.8
Good to soft	168	(16.8)	1000	38.1	29.3
Soft	151	(17.9)	844	32.5	27.4
Heavy	86	(21.0)	409	22.4	35.3
All	**1094**	**(18.8)**	**5828**	**261.6**	**31.4**

For horses which carried 11-10 or more in handicaps. The *expected* number of winners is calculated directly from the number of runners in each race analysed.

The first feature to note regarding Table 9 is that all elements in the first *Difference* column are positive. This illustrates the higher than average strike rate for top weights compared to other runners. The total figure of 261 implies that there were 261 more winners than would have been expected if the horses had been selected at random from all weight bands. Although the figures in the difference column tend to decrease towards the *softer* going categories, this is due to the decline in the number of soft/heavy ground races analysed. In fact, when this effect is removed the pattern becomes quite uniform.

The *Adjusted Difference* column expresses the difference as a percentage of the expected number of winners. In other words, the figures indicate the percentage by which the actual number of winners exceed the expected number. For instance, for the heavy going category there were 29.3% more winners than expected. The high figure for hard going is not particularly reliable due to the small sample size. However, the remaining figures are reasonably uniform. It could be argued that the firm ground figure is high, supporting the case that horses carry weight better on firmer ground, though the good to soft going percentage, at 35.3%, may also be considered high. Consequently, there is no evidence from the above data to conclude that the top weights enjoy a greater advantage over the other runners when the going is firm, and neither are they greatly inconvenienced when the going turns soft.

The final factor to consider under the heading of *Weight Analysis* concerns the effect of course configurations on the ability of the animal to carry weight. It has been suggested that tight turning courses help an animal to carry greater weights since the speed of the runners on these types of track will be lower, on average, when compared to the, so called, galloping tracks. However, justification of this assumption requires accurate definitions of the terms *tight track* and *galloping track*. Ideally, courses would be measured to a reasonable degree of precision, and data relating to the sharpness of the bends recorded. In the absence of these figures, we could use the definitions presented in the official Formbook, or those provided by Timeform to categorise the courses. However, I am not totally happy with these descriptions, which are made, I believe, simply by observation. An alternative approach is to simply analyse all courses individually and base any deductions on these data. The following table lists all National Hunt courses together with the winners to runners strike rate, the average return per £1 staked together with the percentage difference between the number of winners recorded and the number of winners expected for all handicap runners which carried 11-10 or more:

Table 10: Effect of Weight Carried by Course

Course	Winners	(%)	Runners	Average Return/£1	% Diff.
Worcester	57	(23.8)	239	+0.10	79.1
Hereford	34	(23.1)	147	+0.01	75.9
Windsor	19	(20.0)	95	+0.09	74.6
Newcastle	27	(27.3)	99	-0.06	74.0
Perth	30	(28.0)	107	+0.17	65.1
Exeter	37	(21.5)	172	-0.12	56.6
Kelso	25	(23.6)	106	+0.12	54.9
Doncaster	14	(18.9)	74	-0.01	51.5
Fontwell	41	(21.7)	189	-0.14	48.1
Towcester	34	(20.9)	163	-0.03	45.9
Chepstow	29	(22.3)	130	-0.10	43.8
Sedgefield	43	(19.9)	216	-0.17	43.3
Ludlow	23	(16.8)	137	-0.36	42.9
Lingfield	19	(22.6)	84	-0.25	40.0
Bangor	28	(20.9)	134	-0.22	39.9
Nottingham	18	(16.5)	109	-0.03	36.9
Carlisle	21	(20.2)	104	-0.25	35.0
Ayr	32	(21.3)	150	-0.10	34.7
Wincanton	26	(19.8)	131	-0.16	34.5
Plumpton	34	(22.7)	150	-0.26	33.5
Market Rasen	31	(17.5)	177	-0.10	32.3
Ascot	23	(18.1)	127	-0.14	31.3
Southwell	26	(20.8)	125	-0.29	30.9
Wetherby	36	(20.2)	178	-0.17	30.3
Uttoxeter	44	(17.7)	249	-0.20	29.6
Cartmel	9	(20.5)	44	-0.02	23.3

Catterick	14	(14.6)	96	+0.01	21.4
Stratford	30	(16.9)	177	-0.16	21.3
Musselburgh	14	(15.4)	91	-0.26	20.8
Huntingdon	32	(17.7)	181	-0.29	20.1
Haydock	23	(21.3)	108	-0.30	15.9
Newton Abbot	49	(17.9)	274	-0.38	14.5
Newbury	22	(16.9)	130	-0.23	6.7
Kempton	13	(14.9)	87	-0.28	5.7
Warwick	18	(14.4)	125	-0.12	5.0
Hexham	17	(13.5)	126	-0.52	3.9
Aintree	8	(12.1)	66	-0.51	1.5
Cheltenham	24	(13.0)	185	-0.40	0.3
Fakenham	11	(12.2)	90	-0.35	0.0
Folkestone	13	(14.4)	90	-0.47	-4.8
Taunton	14	(9.8)	143	-0.29	-11.1
Sandown	18	(14.2)	127	-0.46	-12.2
Leicester	8	(10.5)	76	-0.48	-22.9

For horses which carried 11-10 or more in handicaps.

Table 10 is sorted by the *percentage difference* column, therefore, the first named courses are best for top weights. Unlike Table 9, there are several negative figures in this column. These indicate the courses where carrying a large weight is actually detrimental to the chances of the horse winning (i.e. fewer horses won than expected). To emphasise this point further, the average return column shows a huge loss of 48p per £1 staked for all bets on horses carrying 11-10 or more in handicaps at Leicester. This compares to a profit of 17p per £1 staked at Perth.

Table 10 is only a guide to the likely effect of racecourse configuration on the chances of the top weights. There are several other factors which have not been considered and which could contribute to the order of the courses given above. For instance, there may be a difference in the average number of runners per race between the tracks which would introduce a slight bias. But more importantly, racing may, in general, be less competitive at some courses with fewer horses carrying large weights per race (i.e. bigger gaps, in pounds, between the top weight and next highest weighted horse). However, if we are prepared to allow for a small degree of error, in what is a very uncertain domain, the results presented in Table 10 should be useful when evaluating the chances of handicappers.

So far we have identified a theory regarding weight carrying which runs counter to conventional logic, and have illustrated that it possesses a degree of merit. Consequently, we should be able to turn this theory into a profitable betting system. The key factors we need to consider are weight carried and racecourse configuration, the going does not appear to have a significant effect.

Using Table 10 it is possible to identify the most successful tracks for top weights. Setting a *percentage difference* threshold at 70% isolates four courses which are considered significantly better for top weights. These courses are: Worcester, Hereford, Windsor and Newcastle. Considering all handicap chase runners which carried 12-0 or more at these courses, starting at less than 10/1, (the reasons for imposing the price restriction have been discussed in previous sections) over the past few seasons would have resulted in 249 bets with 79 winners, a strike rate of 32%, and an average return of 26p per £1 staked. Therefore,

> *consider backing any horse starting at less than 10/1 in a handicap chase at Worcester, Hereford, Windsor or Newcastle which is carrying 12 stone or more: expected profit 26p per £1 staked.*

The evidence published in *Betting For A Living,* based on tests undertaken in the 19th century, indicated that weight only slowed horses to an appreciable degree when the amount reached 14 stone. From the above tables it appears that this argument could still apply today, over one hundred years later.

In summary, the horses which carry more weight win more often. Furthermore, we found that using the weight allotted as an ability rating is as accurate as the tested independent ratings service. The advantage afforded to the top weights does not appear to be reduced when the going turns soft, but can be further enhanced by the configuration of the racecourse.

Front Runners

In the *Beaten Favourites* section we found a profitable betting strategy which ignored current form, and the competition from the other runners in the race. It simply focused on two items of data from the animal's performance history. This does not sit happily with conventional racehorse selection which requires the bettor to evaluate many attributes associated with each runner, such as suitability of going and race distance, in addition to overall level of ability, and then to make a comparison based on these data to determine the most likely winner. However, we found that the *Beaten Favourites* method produces a reasonable profit which is almost entirely due to its unconventional form and the fact that the price at which the horse started in its previous race is not considered to be a significant discriminating factor by most punters and bookmakers. An obvious approach to develop alternative profitable selection methods is to consider other data items which are overlooked by the betting public, and determine their effectiveness at returning a profit. In this section we look at another commonly ignored variable, the style of running and specifically front runners.

In human athletics, other than sprints, front running is not particularly popular. Human middle distance athletes seem to perform better if they are able to run just behind another competitor for the majority of the race. For instance, pace makers are always used for record breaking attempts to ensure that the better athletes do not have to *run from the front*. On the other hand, in horseracing front running is quite popular. This difference could be due to contrasting training regimes or the psychological differences between humans and horses. A human athlete knows the exact distance of the race, the distance he/she has still to run and the fact that the other runners will try to pass him/her. Horses are aware of none of these facts, and are simply running. There are, of course, exceptional cases, where particular horses will not run so well when out in front, and if they are to win need to be held up until the final stages of the race. But in general, horses, without the acute mental awareness of the human athlete, should be able to run just as well, or better, from the front as from any other position in the field.

One popular misconception concerning front runners is the speed they are running relative to the other runners. It is a long held belief by some race observers that front runners are actually running faster than the following pack, and hence the horses which are held up are conserving their energy. If this were true, the gap between the front runner and the pack would be gradually increasing with the front runner drawing further clear. If the gap remains constant, it means that all the horses are running at, or about, the same speed.

There are many advantages to front running which were clearly illustrated by the Martin Pipe - Peter Scudamore partnership during the late 1980s. For example, front runners cannot be brought down. Admittedly, less than 1% of runners are brought down (see Part I) so the advantage is only slight, but nonetheless it is an advantage. Front runners do not suffer from being *unsighted* when approaching a hurdle or fence making the jump much harder to execute and increasing the chances of falling. Master Oats exemplified this point when winning the 1995 Gold Cup. In the initial stages of the race Master Oats was held up behind several horses and his jumping was far from perfect. But as soon as Norman Williamson moved him to the outside his jumping improved markedly and success was virtually assured. Other advantages which can be exploited by the jockey include: taking the shortest route, selecting the best ground on which to race, dictating the pace of the race and, most importantly, starting the race with several lengths lead over the other runners.

So, if we believe that front runners hold a distinct advantage over their competitors, and that this advantage is not universally accepted, we should be able to develop a profitable betting strategy based on this assumption.

Before analysing the data it is important to precisely define the term *front runner* (this aspect of the analysis is covered in detail in the *Developing Profitable Selection Methods* section). From the information in the Formbook, how can we tell if the race was won by a front runner? Clearly, we need to look at the comments-in-running. These comments are designed to provide a brief summary of how the race was run and should contain the information we require. However, analysing these comments is not easy, and in terms of race comments, the definition of a front runner is, to a certain extent, ambiguous. For instance, would a chaser, which took up the lead at the second fence and maintained the lead to the line, be considered a front runner? What about an animal which took up the lead at the third obstacle, was briefly headed two fences out, but regained the lead to win? Obviously, we need to establish a set of rules which satisfy our own definition of a front runner and apply them strictly.

For the purposes of this analysis, I have defined a front runner to be an animal for which the comment-in-running contained either of the following:

made all

or made virtually all

This is very simplistic, and will miss many horses which could be considered to be front runners. However, the definition is unambiguous and can be applied without too much difficulty.

Using this definition about 12% of National Hunt races, in recent seasons, have been won by front runners. This compares to 10% in 1983/84, an increase of about 60 races. Analysing front runners by going should indicate if it is easier to win from the front on certain types of ground. Table 11 presents the number of races won by front runners by going:

Table 11: Analysis of Front Runners by Going

Going	Number of Front Running Winners	Number of Races	(%)
Hard	8	30	26.7
Firm	161	1035	15.6
Good to firm	350	2747	12.7
Good	377	3698	10.2
Good to soft	201	1961	10.2
Soft	209	1914	10.9
Heavy	134	851	15.7
All	**1440**	**12236**	**11.8**

From Table 11 we can see that the proportion of races won by front runners does not vary appreciably (the figure for *hard* going is based on a small sample). And after adjusting for the average field size for each going category, the percentages become even more uniform, leading us to conclude that the type of surface does not affect the chances of a front runner. The conclusion is different, however, when the race distance is considered. Table 12 shows the number of races won by front runners within race distance:

Table 12: Analysis of Front Runners by Race Distance

Race Distance	Number of Front Running Winners	Number of Races	(%)
16f..18f	676	5524	12.2
19f..21f	344	2821	12.2
22f..24f	267	2544	10.5
25f+	150	1313	11.4
All	**1437**	**12202**	**11.8**

Although the percentages appear quite uniform, when they are adjusted for the average number of runners within each race distance category a different picture emerges:

Race Distance	**16..18f**	**19..21f**	**22..24f**	**25f+**
Adjusted %	17.3	15.6	14.5	13.8

It is not surprising to see that front runners win more often in the shorter races. The problem remaining is to convert this information into a profitable selection method.

At this point we need to determine how we will identify probable future front runners. Our current definition only relates to the race in which the horse is running, which is of no use for betting purposes. From a betting perspective, we need to identify *before the race* which horse(s) are likely to front run. Naturally, an animal's past race performances is the best guide. Using the comments-in-running for previous race performances the definition of a likely front runner could have been stated as follows:

> *a horse is identified as a probable front runner if it won its most recent outing and the terms* made all *or* made virtually all *appeared in its comment-in-running.*

Again, this is one of many definitions which could be used and has been selected due to its simple, unambiguous form. Analysing all horses which qualify as probable front runners for four seasons produced the following results: 343 winners from 1225 bets, a strike rate of 28%, with a loss of 17p per £1 staked. This is a very poor result, but with a little refining we should be able to turn this into a profit.

In the previous section we found that horses are able to carry big weights more easily at particular courses. It is also true that front runners are suited by particular types of racecourse, Table 13 illustrates this fact:

Table 13: Average Return and Strike Rate for *Probable Front Runners* by Racecourse

Course	Winners	(%)	Runners	Average Return/£1
Aintree	4	(13.3)	30	-0.52
Ascot	6	(14.3)	42	-0.49
Ayr	3	(15.0)	20	-0.72
Bangor	9	(32.1)	28	-0.17
Carlisle	9	(42.9)	21	+0.12
Cartmel	3	(16.7)	18	-0.72
Catterick	7	(46.7)	15	+1.13
Cheltenham	24	(19.8)	121	-0.30
Chepstow	5	(20.0)	25	-0.53
Doncaster	7	(35.0)	20	+0.75
Exeter	11	(34.4)	32	-0.13
Fakenham	1	(9.1)	11	-0.59
Folkestone	1	(25.0)	4	-0.67
Fontwell	14	(45.2)	31	+0.08
Haydock	9	(23.7)	38	-0.49
Hereford	12	(40.0)	30	+0.32
Hexham	2	(40.0)	5	+0.21
Huntingdon	13	(33.3)	39	+0.13
Kelso	9	(42.9)	21	+0.03
Kempton	18	(32.7)	55	-0.11
Leicester	3	(21.4)	14	-0.52
Lingfield	4	(36.4)	11	-0.17
Ludlow	6	(27.3)	22	-0.53

Market Rasen	8	(25.8)	31	-0.26
Musselburgh	5	(71.4)	7	+1.05
Newbury	10	(23.8)	42	-0.10
Newcastle	4	(19.1)	21	-0.31
Newton Abbot	14	(34.2)	41	-0.31
Nottingham	5	(35.7)	14	-0.07
Perth	8	(47.1)	17	+0.38
Plumpton	13	(40.6)	32	+0.02
Sandown	14	(32.6)	43	+0.27
Sedgefield	6	(25.0)	24	-0.21
Southwell	2	(16.7)	12	-0.38
Stratford	8	(17.4)	46	-0.50
Taunton	6	(25.0)	24	-0.21
Towcester	3	(15.8)	19	-0.70
Uttoxeter	19	(33.3)	57	-0.07
Warwick	8	(25.8)	31	-0.39
Wetherby	8	(19.5)	41	-0.38
Wincanton	7	(28.0)	25	+0.06
Windsor	0	(0.0)	5	-1.00
Worcester	10	(27.0)	37	+0.05
All	**343**	**28.0**	**1225**	**-0.17**

From Table 13 the tracks which suit front runners can easily be seen. The percentage strike rate ranges from 0% at Windsor to 71% at Musselburgh. Consequently, the front runners' courses can be classified by comparing the strike for each track with the overall average strike rate. Setting a threshold at 35%, all courses with a winners to runners strike rate exceeding this threshold would be classified as good tracks for front runners. (This is an arbitrary threshold and can be increased or lowered to vary the analysis.) The courses which exceed the 35% threshold are listed below (excluding Nottingham which no longer stages national Hunt racing):

> Carlisle, Catterick, Doncaster, Fontwell, Hereford, Hexham, Kelso, Lingfield, Musselburgh, Perth and Plumpton.

Backing all qualifying horses at these tracks results in 90 winners from 210 bets, a strike rate of 43%, with an average return per £1 staked of 29p. Therefore,

> *consider backing any horse classified as a probable front runner at Carlisle, Catterick, Doncaster, Fontwell, Hereford, Hexham, Kelso, Lingfield, Musselburgh, Perth or Plumpton: expected profit 29p per £1 staked.*

The above result is quite pleasing. However, it is possible to improve both the strike rate and the average return. Restricting the analysis to handicap races results in 55 winners from 135 bets, a strike rate of 41%, with a return of 43p per £1 staked. We have already seen that front runners are better suited by shorter distance races, and by further restricting our bets to handicap races over 16-18 furlongs improves the return to: 32 winners from 65 bets, a strike rate of 49%, with an average return of 72p per £1 staked.

In summary, horses which have won races by front running are worthy of close consideration. There are many advantages to front running, not least the lead which can be poached at the start of a race. Front runners are better suited to shorter races (i.e. 16 to 18 furlongs), and by particular racecourse configurations.

Sires

In Flat racing the influences of the sire, and to a certain extent the dam, are used to provide clues to the likes and dislikes of the progeny. For instance, as the Derby nears there is always speculation in the trade press regarding the likely levels of stamina possessed by the leading contenders based on the stamina exhibited by their sires, dams and grandsires.

In National Hunt racing, the influence of the animal's parents is not such an important topic. This is because the horses tend to run more often and, hence, their preferences can be determined directly from the form. However, it is a worthwhile exercise to research the influences of the sires of National Hunt horses, and generate information which could be incorporated into betting systems. A full examination of all National Hunt sires is beyond the scope of this book. However, 60 of the top sires have been examined to produce the following tables. The sires quoted are those for whom the influence is significant for each analysis component.

Table 14 illustrates the influence of the sire on its progeny's preference for particular states of going.

Table 14: Average Return and Strike Rate of Progeny's Race Performances by Going

	Fast Ground		Soft Ground	
Sire	**(%)**	**Return/£1**	**(%)**	**Return/£1**
Alias Smith (USA)	4.2	-0.72	12.8	+0.57
Black Minstrel	9.3	-0.46	15.4	-0.21
Blakeney	16.8	-0.02	11.6	-0.47
Broadsword (USA)	10.6	+0.11	4.4	-0.82
Buckskin (FR)	14.4	-0.20	20.5	+0.20
Crash Course	7.1	-0.72	12.6	-0.34
Deep Run	17.7	-0.03	11.6	-0.20
Dominion	11.3	-0.34	16.5	-0.28
Electric	15.6	-0.50	8.4	-0.50
Gunner B	3.8	-0.65	13.3	+0.04
Henbit (USA)	20.4	-0.00	10.8	-0.24
Julio Mariner	15.9	+0.02	7.4	-0.79
Kambalda	22.0	-0.02	12.1	-0.27
Kemal (FR)	11.7	+0.01	16.3	+0.01
Kris	17.5	-0.17	11.9	-0.27
Le Bavard (FR)	14.3	+0.18	6.3	-0.69
Nishapour (FR)	13.2	-0.33	6.6	-0.74
Over The River (FR)	15.4	-0.09	8.6	-0.29
Phardante (FR)	19.1	+0.05	10.7	-0.31
Strong Gale	19.8	+0.01	10.9	-0.39

Torus	16.1	+0.92	11.5	-0.43
True Song	13.2	-0.55	4.5	-0.21
Uncle Pokey	4.0	-0.81	15.6	-0.02

where *fast* ground is defined to be *hard, firm* or *good to firm* and *soft* ground is defined to be *soft* or *heavy* going in the Official Formbook.

There are remarkable differences between some of the percentages presented in the above table. For instance, only 3.8% of the race performances on *fast* going by the progeny of Gunner B have resulted in wins, whereas on *soft* going this figure increases to 13.3%. It is also interesting to note that it would have been profitable to back all progeny of several sires on either soft or fast going. For example, a level £1 stake bet on all the runners sired by Buckskin (FR) would have resulted in an average return of 20p per £1. An analysis by race distance is equally as informative. Table 15 presents this information:

Table 15: Average Return and Strike Rate of Progeny's Race Performances by Race Distance

		Race Distance in furlongs		
Sire		**16..20f**	**21..24f**	**25f+**
Alias Smith (USA)	%	3.5	9.6	17.1
	Ret	-0.49	-0.36	-0.16
Ardross	%	18.9	16.8	12.9
	Ret	+0.19	+0.18	+0.11
Baron Blakeney	%	9.8	9.2	1.8
	Ret	-0.43	-0.44	-0.90
Black Minstrel	%	13.4	11.8	4.9
	Ret	-0.05	-0.27	-0.76
Derring Rose	%	4.0	12.0	17.7
	Ret	-0.84	-0.36	-0.14
Dominion	%	14.7	13.0	7.1
	Ret	-0.29	-0.08	-0.76
Furry Glen	%	15.2	13.4	10.1
	Ret	-0.23	-0.27	-0.38
Green Shoon	%	8.1	9.6	15.4
	Ret	-0.46	-0.43	+0.05
Gunner B	%	10.9	2.6	0.0
	Ret	-0.16	-0.78	-1.00

Le Bavard (FR)	%	7.3	9.2	11.7
	Ret	-0.40	-0.29	-0.43
Oats	%	12.5	14.0	21.5
	Ret	-0.16	-0.16	+0.05
Roselier (FR)	%	12.5	14.4	20.7
	Ret	-0.08	-0.26	+0.50

where *Ret* denotes the average return per £1 staked.

Based on the above data, it is clear that stamina traits are passed from sire to offspring. For example, the progeny of Baron Blakeney do not appear suited by extreme distances in excess of 3 miles. In contrast, the runners sired by Oats seem to excel in long distance races.

A third and slightly more obscure analysis, concerns course directions. Some animals prefer to run in a particular direction, either right- or left-handed. The following table seems to indicate that this preference can be inherited from the sire.

Table 16: Average Return and Strike Rate of Progeny's Race Performances by Course Direction

	Course Direction			
	Left-Handed		**Right-Handed**	
Sire	**(%)**	**Return/£1**	**(%)**	**Return/£1**
Absalom	7.8	-0.69	12.4	-0.44
Ardross	20.3	+0.34	11.4	-0.25
Black Minstrel	9.8	-0.40	15.0	+0.03
Blakeney	9.9	-0.43	15.3	-0.35
Cruise Missile	2.3	-0.57	7.4	-0.69
Furry Glen	15.1	-0.23	11.4	-0.33
Green Shoon	12.4	-0.16	7.8	-0.57
Gunner B	11.0	-0.15	5.3	-0.57
Kemal (FR)	14.4	-0.18	9.8	-0.42
Le Moss	15.4	+0.09	12.6	-0.23
Roselier (FR)	12.7	-0.15	16.5	+0.05
Scallywag	11.0	-0.42	6.8	-0.53
The Parson	15.2	-0.19	11.0	-0.29
True Song	7.4	-0.63	12.2	-0.25
Uncle Pokey	6.8	-0.55	10.9	-0.20

Due to the large number of race performances analysed (over 100,000) all the above differences in strike rate between the course directions are significant. The most striking difference is that for Ardross. A winners to runners strike rate of 20.4% on left-handed courses compared to only 11.4% on right-handed tracks.

The above tables illustrate the traits which can be inherited by horses from their sires. Whilst this information alone cannot be used to formulate a profitable betting strategy, it should be considered as a component of conventional race analysis, especially for previously unraced horses, and to supplement other systematic selection methods.

The Time Factor

In National Hunt racing, previous race times are not generally considered to be of primary importance when analysing races due to the problematic nature of incorporating the data into a sound analytical formula. There are many difficulties associated with using race times to assist in race analysis, specifically the unreliable nature of the going assessments and the variation in the racecourse configurations across the country. However, it is still possible to devise selection methods which rely on previously achieved race times which are worthy of consideration.

The variability of racecourse configuration can, to some extent, be nullified by the introduction of a race standard time. Both the trade papers, as well as Timeform and Raceform, produce standard times for each race distance on every course in Great Britain. Such times are supposed to represent the likely time a horse rated 135 by the BHB would take to run the course on good to firm going. Using these standards facilitates the comparison of race times produced by different horses on different tracks. However it does not take account of varying ground conditions.

Naturally, races run on different ground conditions will produce different times. For instance, races on soft or heavy ground can result in times over 50 seconds slower than the standard, whereas those on a fast surface can be run in times significantly faster than the standard. Clearly, the accurate comparison of such race performances is not an easy problem to overcome.

The calculation of a going allowance, based on the races staged on the course on a particular day, is often suggested as a solution to this problem. This figure can then be used to normalise for the effect of the going at different courses and facilitate the comparison of the race performances. To determine the going allowance, the differences between the actual race times and the standard times are first divided by the race distances and then averaged after any freak figures have been removed.

Therefore, for a six race card, the times may have been as follows:

Table 17: Calculation of Going Allowance

Race Dist.	Race Time (s)	Standard Time (s)	Diff. (s)	Diff. per Furlong (s)
16.5	259.5	237.0	22.5	1.36
20.5	314.5	284.0	30.5	1.49
19.5	316.5	283.0	33.5	1.72
16.5	265.0	228.0	37.0	2.24
24.0	406.4	337.0	69.4	2.89
16.5	260.6	228.0	32.6	1.98

It could be argued that the time for the fifth race is an outlier and should be removed from the going allowance calculation due to its extreme value. Consequently, the going allowance becomes the average of the other five times, namely 1.76 seconds per furlong. In fact, Nick Mordin (in *Betting For A Living*) generally takes the average of the three fastest times excluding any outliers, although there are no hard and fast rules governing the number of races you use.

Once the going allowance has been calculated it is possible to calculate a speed figure for any runner on the card. Firstly, it is necessary to adjust the time of the winner by the going allowance, to produce a normalised time. Therefore, if the going allowance indicates that the track is riding faster than the norm, the winning time is increased accordingly. For instance, if, in a 16 furlong hurdle race, the track is found to be riding 0.1 seconds per furlong faster than the standard, the time of the winner should be increased by 1.6 seconds (i.e. 16 x 0.1). This new time being an estimate of the time the horse would have recorded on average going.

To convert the time to a rating it is necessary to consider the standard race time for the distance. At this point, it is necessary to set the scale for the ratings. Normally, a horse producing a time equivalent to the standard would be given a rating of 100. However, any figure could be used to determine the rating scale. The next step is to determine the difference between the standard time and the adjusted time, in seconds. This figure is multiplied by 5 (lengths run per second). The resultant figure is either added to, or subtracted from, 100 depending on whether the adjusted time is faster, or slower than the standard time. Finally, the figure should be adjusted for distance beaten by the winner. For a more detailed description of calculating speed figures see *Betting For A Living* by Nick Mordin.

Whilst this method for generating speed ratings is well founded in theory, it relies heavily on two potentially unreliable components, namely the standard time and going allowance. In fact, the actual race time itself is far from perfect, depending as it does, in the majority of cases, on hand-timing.

The following method for selecting horses with winning potential utilises the race time and standard time but not the going allowance, which, due to its approximate method of calculation, is the component subject to the highest degree of error.

The selection method is based on the horses which produce the best race times of the day at each racecourse. The *best time* of the day is simply the fastest time relative to the standards. For example, given the six races:

Race Number	Difference from Standard Time (s)
1	+11.8
2	+8.0
3	+2.9
4	+6.2
5	+7.9
6	+5.0

the best race time of the day was recorded in race 3 since this time is closest to the standard and all race times exceeded their comparable standards. In the next example, the best race time was recorded in race 4, the race which produced a time 3.9 seconds faster than the standard (hence the minus sign). The next best time of the day would be race 1 at 1.1 seconds under the standard.

Race Number	Difference from Standard Time
1	-1.1
2	+5.5
3	+2.6
4	-3.9
5	+9.9
6	+11.0

The following table charts the performance of horses which win the race producing the best time of the day, on their next outing:

Table 18: Strike Rate and Average Return for Good Time Performers on Their Next Run

Time[†] Difference	Winners	(%)	Runners	Average Return/£1
0.00-4.00	269	(29.6)	910	-0.01
4.01-5.00	39	(29.3)	133	-0.11
5.01-6.00	25	(31.6)	79	+0.14
6.01-7.00	22	(36.7)	60	+0.48
7.01-8.00	18	(42.9)	42	+0.08
8.01+	24	(31.2)	77	+0.20
Total	**397**	**(30.5)**	**1301**	**+0.03**

† the time difference is the number of seconds between the best time (the qualifying time) and the next best time of the day after adjusting by the standard times.

Clearly, there is some merit in this approach. The strike rate of over 30% is more than adequate. However, an average return of just 3p per £1 staked would translate to a loss for off-course punters. An obvious modification is to restrict the selections to those horses which win races with adjusted time differences of over 5 seconds faster than the next best time of the day. This would result in 89 winners from 258 bets, a strike rate of 34.5%, with an average return of 23p per £1 staked. Therefore,

> *consider backing the winner of the fastest race of the day, providing the adjusted time difference was more than 5 seconds faster than the next best time of the day, on its next run: expected profit 23p per £1 staked.*

It would be logical to conclude that horses in the highest time categories should be the best animals to follow due to their obvious superiority over the other runners at the course. However, the average return for the two highest time categories (i.e. 7.01-8.0 and 8.01+) is, in fact, inferior to the 6.01-7.0 seconds category. One reason for this anomaly is that horses which produce outstanding times, record times etc., are well reported in the press and are brought to the attention of punters and bookmakers. As a result subsequent starting prices for these horses will be reduced to reflect this good performance. An alternative explanation is that such race times indicate errors in the standard time for the course.

An analysis of the 258 selections by race grade should help to improve the average return. Table 19 presents this analysis:

Table 19: Strike Rate and Average Return for Good Time Performers on Their Next Run by Race Grade

Race† Grade	Winners	(%)	Runners	Average Return/£1
Cond. Hdl.	4	(66.7)	6	+2.64
Clm. Hdl.	2	(66.7)	3	+1.67
Nov. Hdl.	14	(38.9)	36	+0.37
Sell. Hdl.	4	(44.4)	9	+2.89
Hcap. Hdl	16	(24.6)	65	-0.01
Hunter Chs.	0	(0.0)	3	-1.00
Cond. Chs.	2	(33.3)	6	-0.48
Clm. Chs.	0	(0.0)	1	-1.00
Nov. Chs.	22	(46.8)	47	+0.23
Sell. Chs.	0	(-)	0	-
Hcap.Chs.	25	(30.5)	82	-0.06
Total	**89**	**(34.5)**	**258**	**+0.23**

† the race grade relates to the race type in which the good time was recorded.

From Table 18 it can be seen that non handicap races seem to provide a better guide than handicaps. By restricting the analysis to non handicaps improves the average return to 58p per £1 staked, although the number of bets is reduced.

In this section we have seen how difficult it is to compare times of different races due to the effect of the going and the wide variety of racecourse configurations. However, it is still possible to develop profitable selection methods using race times and race standards. The method outlined highlights horses which have produced significantly better race times than the other runners on the same card. Whilst these runners are worth following, the level of profitability does not increase linearly with the time superiority. This fact should be remembered when considering backing horses which have produced record times in the past.

Developing Profitable Selection Methods

This final section of Part II is devoted to providing the reader with a set of guidelines for developing, testing and implementing profitable horseracing selection methods.

Development Stage

Simplicity - When designing a selection method it is important not to make it too complex. As the number of variables increases (i.e. distance beaten last time, going last time, going today, race distance last time, race distance today, days since last run etc.) the amount of data needed to give meaningful results increases. Complex systems are also difficult to implement, requiring a great deal of searching through previous form to determine the selection.

Uniqueness - Try to find *new* relationships between the data. Using the normal data items in conventional fashion will, in all probability, produce losing systems. The odds on offer account for the established trends, and consequently there is no value for the punter. For example, Table 6 illustrates the relationship between average return and the distance the horse was beaten on its latest run. For each category of distance beaten within the table the average return is negative. This trend is well known and is fully accounted for in the bookmakers' odds.

Logic - When searching for unique approaches it is imperative to ensure that the variables used are sensible. For instance, whilst backing all horses ridden by bearded jockeys may have returned a profit in the past, facial hair can hardly be considered a reliable discriminating factor with regard to the chances of racing success.

Correlation - Be wary of ill-founded relationships and hidden correlations. As an example, horses running in August tend to produce faster race times than those running in February, therefore they must be better animals. Whilst this conclusion seems a logical deduction from the available evidence, it is an unconsidered variable which produces this result, namely the going. Faster going produces faster race times and the ground is likely to ride firmer in August than February, hence the faster times.

Trainers and Jockeys - Basing systems on trainer and/or jockeys is not particularly reliable for the reasons highlighted in *Correlation*. There is a great deal of correlation between trainers, jockeys and owners: the best jockeys ride for the best trainers and the most dominant owners tend to have their horses ridden by the best jockeys. Consequently, a very profitable selection method can suddenly become very costly if a main owner removes his/her horses from a trainer, or a riding arrangement is terminated.

Measurement - Base the selection methods on quantifiable variables, for example data items such as historical wins to runs strike rate of the horse. Try to avoid qualitative items such as suitability of going, distance etc., unless these terms can be defined precisely. Opinion is difficult to analyse, and it is far from constant. If you feel that suitability of the going is important, then define exactly what constitutes suitable and unsuitable going for a horse. For instance, the following definition could be used for going suitability:

> *the going may be assessed as suitable if and only if the horse has won on an identical surface in the past ten runs.*

However, this in itself will introduce further problems. Using this definition discriminates, to a certain extent, between horses which have won in the past ten runs and those which have not. Consequently, an underlying relationship has already been introduced.

Data Collection - There are three issues concerned with data collection: quality, quantity and spread. Clearly, the data collected needs to be accurate and unbiased. This seems obvious, but it is not necessarily a straightforward task to undertake, especially when extracting data manually from a Formbook. It is very easy to omit particular races during the extraction process reasoning: 'Well, I wouldn't have bet in that race anyway'. Naturally, sufficient data needs to be collected to support the complexity of the system. However, too many seasons' data can introduce bias due to the ongoing changing nature of racing. For instance, in Flat handicaps, horses carrying large penalties were good betting opportunities. However, the introduction of the five-day entry system in 1988 ruined this method. Paradoxically, it is not advisable to extract data from just one season. Certain conditions of the year, weather, quality of horse etc., will bias any analysis. The data needs to be spread evenly over a few recent seasons.

Long Shots - In general, I do not like systems which select long priced winners for two reasons. Developing approaches based on long priced horses requires huge amounts of back data due to the high variance of the average return statistic. In fact, if a selection method has selected a long priced winner (i.e. 20/1 or greater) I remove it from the analysis. It only takes one or two of these selections to turn a very poor system into a seemingly profitable method. Furthermore, when running the system these selections are often ignored, especially during long losing runs.

Strike rate - Aim for an approach with a reasonable winner to bets strike rate. A strike rate of just 10% is not really high enough, the losing runs will occur too frequently and could be extremely long. Aim for a strike rate of at least 20%.

Testing Stage

There are two different ways of testing a new selection method. The first involves partitioning the data set *before* the development process. One part can be used for development and the other for testing. For instance, if the data have been collected from four seasons, the first three seasons could be used to develop and refine the system with the fourth season used for testing. The second method, and the one I prefer, is to test the system live. In other words, develop the approach on all available and relevant data, and conduct the testing phase during the following year by either keeping a record of the system's performance or by actually backing the selections to small stakes. In addition to providing a real test environment, this approach is also one of education for the punter. By closely monitoring the system through the placement of bets, the punter will get a better *feel* for the method and perhaps identify other highly correlated variables. For instance the likelihood of long losing runs, the way he/she reacts after several losing bets etc. Once satisfied with the validity of the system the punter can then increase the stakes.

Running The System

It is very easy to break the rules of the system, especially during long losing runs. This behaviour should be avoided. Providing the system has been based on well-founded ideas, and has been adequately tested, there is no need to doubt its ability to return a profit. Consequently, the devised staking plan should be adhered to. There is nothing worse than finding, at the end of the year, that you have lost money, and that if you had kept to the system's rules you would have made a profit.

CONCLUDING REMARKS

Throughout this book I have attempted to show that whilst it is possible to make a profit from Jumps racing, it does not necessarily come from the conventional approach to winner finding. Simply backing a high proportion of winners does not ensure a long term profit.

The conventional approach to race analysis requires the punter to determine, amongst numerous other factors, whether the selection is suited by the race distance, going, track configuration etc., all of which have been considered by the bookmakers before pricing up the race.

Consequently, punters and bookmakers are working with the same data, and if they both adopt similar approaches to solving the race surely the punter must come off worse in the long run. A good example concerns the selection method based on time. Horses which produce outstanding times are not as profitable to follow as those which merely produce good times since this fact is widely reported and reflected in subsequent starting prices. A good, but not record breaking time, is often overlooked by bookmakers and not incorporated into the price assessment.

So how can the punter make a profit? Well, there are three options. The first requires the punter to become so knowledgeable about horseracing that his/her assessment of the true probabilities is vastly superior to the bookmakers', to bet only on-course (avoiding tax) and always get the best price. This is asking a great deal, but it is achievable. The second option is to acquire information that is unknown to the public and bookmakers. For instance, to know when a fancied horse is not trying. However, I expect that such information would not come cheaply. The third option is to adopt a different perspective on race analysis, and use information which is not normally considered, to form alternative selection methods which return long term profits.

Over many years I have tried the first and second approaches to backing horses, although recently I have relied almost entirely on the systematic approach. Occasionally, tempted by the sound theoretical basis of conventional race analysis, I attempt to *study form*. However, I usually regret these lapses.

Whether you choose to adopt a systematic approach to betting or not I hope that you have found some worthwhile material in this book to incorporate into your betting strategies.

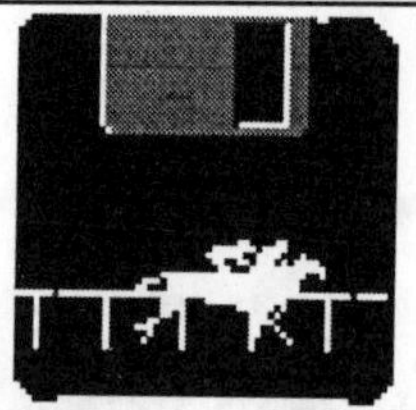